DATE DUE

18 2008

Demco, Inc. 38-293

CONVERSION

Poems by

REMICA L. BINGHAM

Lotus Press
Detroit

First Edition

ISBN: 978-0-916418-98-4
ISBN: 0-916418-98-7

Printed and manufactured in the United States of America

Cover design by Leisia Duskin

Lotus Press, Inc.

"Flower of a New Nile"

Post Office Box 21607
Detroit, Michigan 48228

www.lotuspress.org

For my parents

ADVANCE PRAISE FOR *CONVERSION*

"I think it will be Remica Bingham's war poems that will spread the rumors that you can download this book to some gadget in your pocket. Let's hope so. *Conversion* is a book you might want to wave inside your church. Black life still glitters when Black poets speak. Remica Bingham is a poet writing poems that fan themselves with joy. It would be a sin not to take this book home."

— E. Ethelbert Miller

"Remica Bingham is a true prodigy in the best sense of that word, for her youth belies the singular voice, the craft brilliantly apparent in these poems of longing and faith — and her fear is nonexistent, even when she walks the prophet's awful ground. What epiphany, what beauty! *Conversion* is a promise kept, the evidence of things unseen."

— Honorée Fanonne Jeffers

"Remica Bingham is a startlingly original and groundbreaking voice — sassy and pinpoint, with an obvious reverence for both innovation and craft. While it's possible to memorize the workings of poetry, to talk the talk and analyze the genre to its very bones, Bingham is that rare creature who instinctively breathes as a poet breathes. Not many of us will live long enough to see the world as she does — as a limitless canvas brimming with stories she simply must tell. And she tells them as no one else can. I am enriched, encouraged and ultimately enlightened by the lyricism and electricity in this work, and have no choice but to offer the ultimate compliment. I wish this voice was mine."

— Patricia Smith

"These poems help me withstand the weight of things that shape my life. What else is poetry for — if not to allow moments of mutual recognition, moments when our various solitudes no longer seem impenetrable but understood and shared. Remica Bingham's new poems offer again and again that satisfying feeling that comes when you recognize your own better and enlivened self in the words of someone else. This is a wonderfully engaging debut."

— Tim Seibles

*"Love does not begin and end
the way we seem to think it does.
Love is a battle, love is a war;
love is a growing up."*

–James Baldwin

Contents

I

This Could Be the Reason

I leave my shoes
all over the house—
sneakers cast
from the empty kitchen
to the not-so-good-for-living room,
winter boots lined, waiting
in the laundry room behind the Gain,
slippers wedged between
the bursting bookcase
and worn couch.

You should pick up your shoes
my grandmother says
hide 'em under your bed.
You ain't careful,
somebody's gonna see
where you been, tell you
just where you goin'.

Sighting

The night my father appeared
at our kitchen window,
his face touching the pane,

I was six and screamed like I'd seen the ghost
of a man killing himself with cocaine and distance.
He vanished so quickly I had only enough time

to tell my mother, watch her run
to the side door and listen to footsteps
crushing leaves in the backyard.

She waited—his shadow darkened
the glow of the farthest streetlight—
then bolted the door, turned away.

For weeks I sat hinged on the windowsill,
eyes probing, craven, hopeful;
hand pressed against the still cold glass.

Portrait of Mother's Kitchen

Kettle the color
>   of Augusta tadpoles
marred by chicken grease and unkept steam
black handle
>   worn smooth

Hotcomb resting
>   on the leftback burner
stove eye red   glaring
remnants of scalp and ears charred
>   between metal teeth

Dead mouse
>   in the corner
right side of its head stuck
to a square glue trap
>   tail tucked under hind legs
>   pupils bulging glossy blind

Spider plant
>   in the square window
creeping toward Dollar Store curtains
pressed thin
>   gleaming
>   floor lit with the smell of pine

5

A Friend Explains the Second Coming

Eugene said his mother was Jesus
and meant it, leaning into tears.

The only ransom he knew, she took
her life with forged prescriptions

and a wide determined swallow.
He always tells the story of her coming

to St. Pius private school, gripping a baseball bat
the day some chump threatened him with agnostic fists.

You swing, I swing was all she had to say
staring into the bully's glistening eyes.

He loved her most like that, full of fire and brimstone,
charged with the salvation of her first-born son.

Now she appears in his dreams—luminous and transformed—
bat in hand, swinging home.

Ornithology

You're too young to know
I helped raise finches, little birds that needed mates to live,

fed them with my hands, then let them flutter
from their cage, alighting on bedposts, dressers, lamps.

They are long gone. One caught a cold
and, in days, was buried beneath the steps of my apartment.

In less than a week I found the other,
a stiff feathered ball, curled inside their water-dish.

When you entered our lives—tiny, blinking
grump of a man, already coarse with the world—

I chirped out songs until you watched, wide-eyed, the familiar hymn
I'd practiced against your mother's stomach, serenading her womb.

Your recognition—awed silence, miniature hand
encircling my finger—made clear

for the first time how one small thing
couldn't live without the other.

Even as a fledgling in this world, testing your wings
you taught me. Listened, as I sang my love.

Initiation

Rushed from the pediatrician's
puzzles and Highlights magazines
to the gynecologist's cervical charts,
STD pamphlets, stirrups.

Tomboy punches to her chest
replaced by underwire and straps;
her see-thru Barbie backpack now
a leather purse with clandestine zippers.

Her first march through the drugstore spawned
tales of belts and rags. New vocabulary—tampon,
maxipad—and words she knew given new meanings—
overnight, heavy, Always—these she refused to carry.

She's a tough one her Gran said, combing out
her pigtails, pressing untamed tresses flat.
Sit still her mother hissed, popping her swinging legs
with a thin plastic comb.

Finally, she sat—ankles crossed, hands folded.
How do I know if I feel like a woman?
Does it hurt? they asked.
Well she said *not*
between my legs.

Fish Fry

My family sits around the table
sharing fried fish and a bushel
of June's first crabs,
all female and tender.
I eat only legs, watching one uncle
break back upon back with his teeth,
not stopping for claw or egg or eye.

You want a hand in the pot
but won't dig for the meat
he says to me.
You got to get it all,
suck it 'til it's dry.

I look at my aunt who said she'd stayed
for the children after the first affair
because she was *just too tired* after the sixth.
My cousin, pregnant, cursing
all men in lieu of the one
she can no longer find.

One by one I count, the transgressed
and transgressors, the men, laughing
chiming *Uh-huh, that's right*
and all the empty shells of women—
heads down, eyes tame as those
in our hands.

Gratitude

Each time I enter Autumn Care Nursing Home
residents line the glistening beige tile.

I walk past the nurses' station—three, on duty, sitting
behind the glass. None moving to see why Mr. Trueblood is screaming

Help me, please, help me. He has dropped an orange.
His mouth twists small and silent when I put it in his hands.

My grandmother is usually sleeping, eyes dimmed to a slit,
T.V. blaring, arms dangling, hands limp.

I touch her shoulder and she wakes giving orders—*Get my shoes;
brush my teeth; take out my bible, leave it in my reach.*

I move around her half of the square room
until she can think of just one other task,

the only order she doesn't give aloud—
her head nodding backwards, her eyes on my hands.

I slide behind her wheelchair and draw the curtain separating her
from Ms. Williams who suffers with dementia and yells

Oh, I know what you're doing as we disappear.
I remove my grandmother's blouse, unfasten her bra and slide

my nails from the nape of her neck down to her buttocks
until white lines, like lightning, cover her skin.

10

She is silent. This tells me I am finally doing something useful.
I warm lotion with my palms and lather it onto her back until she says

what I came to hear—*That feels some kinda good*—her gratitude:
measured and easy. My acceptance: each day's return.

On Behalf of Frye's Grocery and the O'Jays

For the Post-it notes you left in my lunchbox,
the folded construction paper hearts after
we'd gone to bed angry at each other;
the Pillsbury chocolate chip cookies
and Subway Club sandwich that made me the envy
of every child before field trips;
for the Silly String and water balloon grenades
you planted beneath my Capri-Sun
on the last day of school;
for the Doritos and double-deckers stacked
with Boar's Head turkey and cheddar
when you had a boiled egg, grapefruit (from the neighbor's tree)
and water at 3 a.m., your only break on the graveyard shift;
for the Hostess cupcake with cream filling
and white icing swirl when you had
no sugar except my morning bliss;
for the three-second symphony that read:
You're my darlin', darlin' baby,
for the Revlon Cocoa Vaughn kiss that followed.

Gesture

On our way to Sunday breakfast
my father and I see a man
wearing a hooded sweatshirt and workpants
stained with white paint and mud.

He is sluggish at 7 a.m., a slight
scowl on his face, right hand
clutching a large book
as if it were his child.

As we pass by—our car months old
and freshly washed, my father's suit
starched, handkerchief creased—the man
lifts his eyes and head, softly jutting his chin.

Watching the exchange—my father's return
nod and raised wrist, fingers bent almost
into a fist—I ask *Do you know him, Daddy?*
wondering, *Have you been him before?*

Mercy Killing

At Big Ma's, I stood in the middle of each room,
careful not to lean on walls or too near closets,
afraid the vermin—now outnumbering
the hairs on her head—would find their way
to my purse or pockets.

When asked to go to her drawer for antacid, I hesitated
knowing I'd have to reach in amidst their dark scattering
to soothe her. *These are the sacrifices we make*
my mother said while on the floor at Big Ma's feet,
clipping her toenails, using a slipper
to smash roaches as they came.

My father hated the dirtiness of any place
yet knelt, in his finest charcoal suit, near the phone cord —
twisting its disconnected wires—
surely aware of the thick dust graying his elbows and knees.
Until he heard a dial-tone and Big Ma said
I can call now if I need you, he did not rise.

Hours later, in public with our private lives well-clothed,
when I saw the silvery-brown pest slip
from his pants cuff—remembering my parents' selflessness,
their hushed mercy—I used my sharp-tipped shoes
to make a sacrifice and killed it—quiet, swift—without mentioning
my fear and without his ever knowing.

The Seams of Memory

The woman said she mistook Mike
    for a trashcan when she barreled through night, her sedan

lifting him into darkness. He fell, head first,
    back to the asphalt he'd been trying to escape for years

and my father—a friend who knew
    Mike's worth—clamped his hands

around Mike's open head, pressing until
    he could no longer see the orange-gray meat.

My father held that broken man lying between white lines
    on a dark New Jersey street, cradled him

and rocked until paramedics came to sew
    the seams of his memory back together.

Months later, those same hands would cut Mike's hair
    and watch for stitches, carefully shearing the past away.

The News in Spring

Words battle the car stereo, rushing air, evening traffic—
what good is the approaching summer, what good the trip
east and uncle's open arms at Gate 40, Terminal B,
what good the shared straw in a Watermelon Freeze
passed between rocking chairs at Friendly's, what good
his homeruns on Red Bank Field two blocks
from Count Basie Theater, what good the live jazz
Friday evenings on the water, what good the crisp
twenty dollar bill pressed into my palm for
whatever, those books you like, what good the stories
about his escapades, his four women at my parents'
wedding, what good the mystery, the rumored
clairvoyance, birth with a veil and two teeth,
what good his premonitions when—*Your uncle*

Ralph

AIDS

Taxidermy to Ashes

Crystal's parents were taxidermists,
their shop full of stuffed heads,
wood and thread

The first time she invited me there
I was shocked to see death
displayed so freely—it was hidden
at all the houses I knew

> My parrot bundled,
> buried in the grass.
> My hamsters, who ate the plastic
> soapdish and the food it held,
> floated in a box upstream.
> My seven goldfish, all
> flushed privily while I slept.

When I told her of the urn that held
both my uncles' ashes, she never
asked me over again

She said   *I just can't imagine
the way you treat your dead*

The Last Night of Fire

Each evening when we were twelve
my friends and I crowded one two-story stoop
until streetlights flickered, signaling our bolt home.

One kid, Wyatt, whose father
was the oldest dealer on the block—a fact
we never mentioned because overlooking
is the only way, somtimes—suggested
practicing for drive-by shootings in case an initiation
took place on our street, our staircase fingered as the target.

Brent—the boy who could summon the best rendition
of gunfire—shot off rounds with his mouth and we took cover
shrouding ourselves with the thin metal beneath the steps.
We huddled and giggled until the timekeeper announced
thirty seconds and all ten of us rose like dust.

One night, it started. By morning, we peered into holes
on our stoop, inspecting the chipped paint
falling from stucco walls. The second night,
they riddled light-posts, windows and sides of cars.
Before school, we removed bullet shells
from the litter box Ms. Garcia kept on her porch,
though she'd had no cat for years.

The third night, they came just after dark.
Louis—notorious for lingering—heard quick fire,
ducked behind a tree and crawled under the steps
whispering our playtime warning *stay low, stay low.*

With his knees and stomach pressed to the dirt, he began counting.
He was on 19 when he heard tires screeching
and continued—*20, 21, 22*—until he reached 30,
even then he couldn't stop.

Two hours had passed when his mother went searching,
recognized the only nameless tennis shoes she could afford
protruding from beneath the stoop and leaned closer, flinching
when she saw him—knees bloodied, tear-soaked face,
lips trembling with numbers.

II

Potter's Field

grand father's plow

empty well   forty-nine acres

banker's note   unpaid debt

30,000 regrets

loose barn door   broken handle

child's handwriting   on the wall

shed light   without a fixture

burdened beasts   lost atonement

beneath calloused hands

fingerprints resting   on the coat of a lamb

rabid dog   slaughtered calf

barren ewe

Birth and Burden,
Scotland Neck, North Carolina, 1922

You are bearing the child of a man
who has given you nothing
but the fruitage of his devilish ways.

Even now—as his child
mangles your insides, as your teeth
find lip's flesh—he is at a gambling house
in the backwoods, nursing his last lucky hand.

You are used to emptiness but still
reach out. He is miles away, cradling
a pot of dirty money filled by the others—
angry and itching—around the table.

As a fist rips your womb, he also suffers
a blow. Fresh blood races along his temple where a bullet
has skimmed past reason into night.

This and only this pushes him back to your marriage bed,
grunting when he spies his daughter suckling
your breast under patched, bloodied sheets.

He faces the coming morning, his back
to both of you, his aching head attached
to the one body crowding your peaceful room,
his pockets full with indifference.

1955: Snapshot in Black and White

My last day in Europe
we took pictures on the border
between Germany and Austria,
her chocolate hair
blocking out the sun,
ivory hands fingering the trigger
and lens.

Afterwards, we held one another
in the backseat of her Opel
like teenagers leaving for college.
Overlooking the mountains
we'd seen each morning
from her kitchen window,
I watched her watching me —
only loss shadowing her face.

Lying in her bed that night
I thought of Willie back home,
caught looking at Mister Whitlock's
daughter prancing in the lake.
His mama wouldn't even grab his coat
before rushing him to a train
heading North, saying *Boy,*
you better off cold, than dead
leaving him in the porters' hands and God's.

Marchers Headed for Washington, Baltimore, 1963

On Sunday—the amen-scent of fresh meat, apples
bearing nutmeg, collards simmered vinegar-sweet.

For days my father's mother let dawn rub
the back of her neck and shoulders, rising
in time to see the moon.

On Monday—fried chicken battered
with whole flour and double-A eggs,
seasoned with onion salt and lemon pepper.

As shards of light brightened
the darkest spot in her kitchen—the deep
slit that held last winter's preserves—she'd leave her work
and enter the bedroom her four sons shared.

On Tuesday—fresh Virginia ham, sliced thick,
sweetened with maple sap turned molasses.

Wiping at the sleep clouding their eyes,
one by one her boys marched
to the closet searching for the starched sets
of hand-me-down Sunday best awaiting them.

On Wednesday—pot roast and hotwater cornbread,
the cornmeal sifted as fine as loose road dust
lifting to settle on trousers and lace socks.

If all was right—each bowtie and collar
securely in place—she would line them up
in seats on the porch—even the youngest,
not yet five—then kneel, daily, offering
brief instructions: *Listen, children, and watch.*

On Thursday—smoked turkey, bronzed with heavy
brown sugar, stuffed with new potatoes and corn.

When the morning cooking was done and more
waited in pots atop the stove for the afternoon,
she began piling plates so high
they had to be doubled, covered in foil
and set in brown paper bags strong enough
to endure fifty more stone-ridden miles.

On Friday—fish and loaves, tanned backs of whiting
and yeast rolls passed from hand to hungry hand
until each passerby signaled enough.

When travelers approached, the first son
to spot them would stand and shout, *Here two come,*
Mama—or three or four, even nine came
into view once. Rushing to the door with arms
outstretched, he'd clutch the plates warming
his small hands, then go to the roadside with her message:

This is for the journey, my mama said,
in hopes that none of you will ever stop.

She fed hundreds that way, never seeing
any face close enough to recall it
clearly, her name unknown by those saying grace.
Her marching—from kitchen to porch, then
steadily, back and back again—all but in place.

The Third King Dreams of Assassination

"Do not become fearful of those who kill the body
but cannot kill the soul . . ." – *Matt. 10:28*

Too young at ten
to make the distinction
between names, if they said
Martin I thought of myself,
didn't know they were speaking
to the man I called Daddy,
thought people were calling to me.
Crowds shouted   *Be safe Martin!*
Martin look out! So I did,
each day certain
there was a bounty
on my head.

When they shot my father
I worried that someone would harm me,
not because of my skin but my name.
A year later, we found my uncle
floating in a pool. His lungs were as dry
as his unused towel
when they pronounced
drowning his cause of death.
Hate changed for me then.
Everyone was dangerous,
everyone in danger.

I woke wary of men with hands
disappearing into coats, angry

29

women wielding knives.
Solace only came
in my Father's house.
I'd heard of four little girls lost
in Bombingham, voters dragged
from booths in Zion, but didn't think
the devil had enough gall
to come calling there.

One sticky Sunday in June, I sat
listening to my grandfather's sermon
when a new parishioner stood and aimed
what looked like a small black bible
as my grandmother wrapped her voice
around The Lord's Prayer.
I saw the front of her white dress
billowing red and knew
they had missed me again.

I turn to Matthew over morning coffee
and with bourbon before bed,
but am not wholly convinced.
I fear every man who reaches out
to touch me, every stone
thrown in my path.

With Ease

He never mentions waking up to frost glossing his window,
his father throwing logs into the cast iron stove, his mother
cooking Scrapple and fried eggs for breakfast.

How it took hours to make sure his two brothers
and one sister all had their hats, gloves and books,
longer on mornings when one slumped to the ground
in tears because he'd worn another
hole in the sole of his boot or when his sister
cornered their mother, begging for Ivory
instead of Octagon because some high-yellow
girl at the park called it *nigger soap.*

He got all four of them, plus two cousins and one friend,
eight miles from their clapboard homes in Park Place
to Jacox Elementary—the only school they were allowed
to attend—on time, every day of the school year.

No yellow buses came across the tracks, but just after sunrise
there was a thirty-car coal jack—a Northwestern train
filled with black diamonds heading south.
They'd strap their books around their backs
and stand as if on the starting line, close enough
to feel the welcome rumble before
they saw oncoming light.

As it came into view, he'd count them off—
One, two, three, go! and she'd jump. *Four five, six, go!*—
until each child grabbed hold of the rail and looked ahead.

He laughs aloud telling it now—his body rocking with ease
like a buoy, his arms raised as if in mid-Sunday morning shout—
how his were the last hands to touch the cold metal,
his feet always the last to leave the ground.

My Mother Recalls Protests

Not the news of it:

    how the city would level the three-tiered building where six
    of her siblings marched in burgundy caps and gowns—
    all bought with quarters her mother set aside each week.

But the actual movement:

    students bused away from their homes and Champs Restaurant
    across the street—the red grand-opening ribbon cut by Ali, after he'd
    shaken hands and thrown air-jabs, running through their auditorium.

Not the way they came:

    hundreds of high school kids storming black middle schools.
    Their marching like thunder, their pouring through halls
    and classrooms like summer rain after drought.

But the way children followed:

    battling teachers then climbing through first-story windows.
    Their stride—like Daniel's into the lion's den. Every student rising
    from a desk or swing set an Elijah called away to peace.

Not the sight of those she knew:

    her friend Michael—whose bible-toting mama chased him down
    the street after hearing he'd cut school then had the nerve

33

to stand in front of City Hall chanting *Hell no! We won't go!*
on the six o'clock news.

But one boy no one recognized:

who—instead of shouting in unison with the crowd—ran screaming,
shaking like a man consumed with fire. His distorted face clouding
the camera, his high-pitched refrain: *Where else can we go?*
What else do we have?

After Hurricane Isabel,
Residents of Public Housing Interpret Signs

The storm split eighty trees, their limbs
    cast shadows on walls of parks:
For days, tenants saw black Jesus,
    his night-lit face blessing Roberts Park;

One homeless man, gagged by police,
    howled sullied warnings. Baptizing his tongue
in corn liquor, he screamed fire—
    what he thought he saw—singeing Diggs Park;

Four horses and riders, three sets of six
    lines and Lucifer's torrid grin—
five families fled the signs
    of the beast darkening Bowling Park;

A Yoruba priest came seeking gods and prayed
    for children captured in stone.
When he told mothers dead sons could return,
    hymns flooded Tidewater Park;

They said, *Come see Jesus, fires, the end,*
    but I wouldn't follow new prophets,
plain men—wary of slick, fleeting phantoms
    gracing blocks in each park;

An autistic child became clairvoyant,
    offering midnight omens—clawed
at her father's ghostly face. Still
    no one has seen him in Moton Park;

35

An old mid-wife saw ninety-eight births then
     nothing on smoke-colored brick.
Days before she'd turn ninety-nine,
     her sluggish procession filled Young Park;

Now during tempests, I'm a baptized believer,
     seeking out light-ravaged walls.
Wait for shadows to whisper my name,
     as night falls christening these parks.

Sergeant C. Rosales III

I. 1994: Cecilio *I-Sincere*

Two years my senior,
awkward kid with thick glasses and slight
Panamanian accent, took his nickname
from a relative who moved
kilos in north Jersey

When my cousin called me
fat girl   bookworm   Cecilio didn't
crack a smile, just handed me
his glasses and wrestled my offender
to the blue-checkered tile floor

He'd sit in Nana's kitchen
watching me eat fresh peaches,
juice sliding down my chin and neck,
until the dam broke on his foreign tongue:

Usted es la mujer de mis sueños,
venido vaya con mí por favor
I spoke no Spanish, but understood
every word

He hid me in his bedroom loft
closed his eyes and whispered
May I before lifting my blouse

II.   1997: Missing Home

He rubbed my back for two hours
one stormy day in August.
I'd left the cacti, scorpions and Phoenix
sun before monsoons could come
to wash things clean.
In a darkened room, under a blanket
of New Jersey rain, I wept
into the only comfort I'd had in weeks—
the warmth of his hands
on my shoulders, neck and waist
circling *sleep, sleep, sleep.*

III.   1999: Nationalism

You give too much
I told him
when he explained the marriage
taking place in two days, one month
before high school graduation

Her green card would come
in two years,
the divorce planned
before the wedding

It's hard being in a country
that isn't your own
and wanting to stay

His way of saying
I would never understand

IV. 2001: Forward March

The military paid
more than college.
He'd *be all*
he could be
for a few years, anyway,
save enough
to start a family
someday

The marriage ended.
To pass enlistment time
spent far from home, he dated
someone new—a sweet
Samoan girl who massaged
his feet at night

She's pregnant
he whispered
Do you love her
I asked

You were right
he said
This could be
too much

V. 2002: Operation Iraqi Freedom

He chose ground infantry
for the $10,000 bonus
but never thought
he'd be shipped to Iraq
seven months
after his only
child was born

His family watches CNN
praying and scanning lists:
casualties   wounded   prisoners of war

looking for plastic-rimmed glasses
behind journalists   searching
for a glimpse of auburn
skin and small pointed nose

His daughter
has learned one word
Dada
in his absence

VI.   2003: Letter Haiku

In February
he wrote *I won't be long*, had
settled in by June

Spoke of stars in March,
clear nights when choking red dust
didn't cloud his dreams

Could count the lives he'd
taken by April, faceless
men bloodied his hands

By May, guilt set in.
He pondered the power of
grenades, his handgun

Thirteen desperate men
stepped on mines in June, longing
for any way home

Sent dinars bearing
Saddam's sneering face, in July,
worthless bills filled streets

His last letter came
near August, weeks later than
his quiet return

VII.   2004: Homecoming

He came back
with a wallet full
of what he'd seen

I looked closely
at each print
searching for the change
in him

Why the guns,
begging children,
men, blindfolded, on their knees?
I asked and studied
his unfamiliar face
in each picture,
things were missing.

Where are your glasses?
He misunderstood.
Said he broke them
in an exchange of fire

I wanted to know
if he could still   see

43

Minutes, Abu Ghraib Prison, October 18th, 2003

I. US Soldier, 12:06 p.m.

In the latrine, slipping off my panties,
I think back to what my mother told me
the first time I'd been with a man,
then again the day I enlisted.
You can give him everything
and he'll find ways
to ask for more.

II. POW, 11:43 a.m.

I am naked, being straddled by a small woman.
The velcro on her pants scratches my thighs;
she rakes her fingernails across my skin.
I couldn't have wanted this,
even if she were not my enemy and young enough
to remind me of my eldest daughter.
I have never been beneath a woman
I tell her with my eyes, my lips pursed
with curses, tongue thick with prayer.

III. US Soldier, 12:09 p.m.

I consider rinsing them in the metal sink
before stuffing them in my jacket pocket.
Sergeant said to bring them back
quick, he needed more props.
All the world's a stage, I think, remembering
a line from my high school play last spring
then alter my face, check the dull mirror for
anger, conceit, no shame.

44

IV. POW, 11:47 a.m.

When he orders her *up and off*, I see him
pull her aside. His teeth almost touch
her ear as he whispers, his hand cups
the small of her bottom. I watch them
until she catches my gaze—
a smile softening her hard cheeks. I search her
mouth for mercy, but find
spit glazing my chin, nose and lips.

V. US Soldier, 11:51 a.m.

If there were room for weakness
none of us would make it home.
I can't think of this man's family—the children
holding fast to his arms and legs
in the picture we took from his pocket.
Instead, I think of the other photo—his family's men
aligned on the grass, behind them only fragments
of women. I counted five heads, two elbows,
one shoe and think of how he'd treat me
if I were his silent wife—the woman
almost bowing behind him. No mercy, just
fire leaves my mouth.

VI. POW, 12:12 p.m.

How can I return home
having felt an unbridled woman,
having had soldiers clip leather
around my neck and tug
until I rose to my feet, having
heard the click of their cameras,

their laughter, having seen her return
patting a lump on her chest and pull out
cotton briefs much like the ones my wife wears to bed,
having swallowed the stinging
acid in my throat, having endured
her hands stroking my bare chest, having suffered
unnatural blindness as she placed her underwear
over my head like a *hijab*?

Hijab – traditional head covering worn by Muslim women.

Simmie Knox Paints Bill Clinton
for the White House

I was born in 1935 in Aliceville, Alabama, a sharecropper

During planting season,
I would stand at the end of each tilled row
until I could see a picture
of what was to come—ripe bolls of cotton
held up by browning cups and stems.
At sundown, I'd go back to the house
and draw the opposite of what I knew.
That's where I learned to use my hands
for work.

When I don't know you . . . I'm really feeling in the dark

My aunt asked me to paint her father,
the first man buried in our family plot, his soaked back
bent over a horseless plow ablaze in my fingers.
I could paint my aunt twelve years after
she'd been dead because I could still see her
pushing the store-bought paper and watercolors
into my sixteen-year-old hands, telling me my gifts
were also God's—resurrection, eternal life.

but all I need is one good exposure

I took sixty pictures, even after shaking his hand.
We talked about growing up in the South
in turbulent times but remembered things

47

differently. I thought of Woolworth's bloodied
counters the day a college friend was dragged
from his stool. He thought of the doors, locked
and bolted after, how he had to walk twelve blocks
for candy.

We both know what it's like to be deprived of things

When he mentioned never knowing his father—
killed three months before his birth—I put my camera
down. He said his mother gambled and ran
into the strong arms of an alcoholic. Twice that man had drawn
a gun on them and hit him once with the butt of it.
I thought of my own fading mother then and finally
saw him clearly. His face creased and stained as any other
human face. I picked up my brush.

Can you imagine that?

O'Connor's South

I.

I read a sign aloud that said
Open air fires unlawful before 4pm
while driving through Emporia
with Princess and Til. We laughed until
someone said   *That's why you never see
crosses burning before evening,* half-smiling,
as we made our way further South.

II.

When we sped by—three brown women staring,
my right pointer aimed at a black-faced lawn jockey
decorating a sweaty white man's lawn—the man, out gardening,
snapped his neck to watch. At the stop sign not twenty feet
from his azaleas, I looked back, am sure I saw him
lean toward his 'artificial nigger' and whisper.

III.

Ice-cream seemed the only thing cool enough
to combat South Carolina's September swelter,
but the marquee at Dairy Dream didn't advertise
two scoops for the price of one or free sprinkles.
Suffering truth decay it read—light reflecting
the Baptist steeple towering across the street—
Read your Bible. Get a treat.

IV.

In hours, my grandfather would bury his mother
and wanted a bulb for her porchlight, left burning

for elderly guests paying respects
in the night. When he asked for 75 watts,
the man behind the counter gave him 40.
My grandfather pointed out the difference
but the man didn't budge, just asked   *Boy,*
what ya'll need all that light for?

III

Topography

Tonight   I'm moving,

　　　　　　　　　traveling beyond modern mumbling

　　　　　　　　　　　to a prehistoric groan.

　　Before fillers and fidgets

　　　　　　　　was the guttural hum,

the soft skin of thigh

　　　　　　　　　　under rough begging hand.

　　　　　　　Before we began paraphrasing want,

there were tongues with purpose, topography

　　　　　　　for mouth and underbelly, dams

for the body's rivers.

　　　　　　　　　　　My breasts are tender

　　　　for the wrong reasons—not

　　　　　　　　insistent teeth, unyielding

jaw or kneading hand—they ache from the lack

　　　　　　　　　　of honest touch.

Keep watching

and I'll open my body like Solomon

serenading Shulamite daughters

of distant lands.

If evidence is

what you want

get the pomegranate wine, choose

any appendage as a reed-brush pen.

Sign here.

Adam's Conversion

It must put danger
in your relationship
if you're the last
creature on the planet
to get a mate.

When that day came
you'd gladly mask
the ache in your side
and vow allegiance
to her creator.

After the snake appeared
walking upright and speaking
in the tongue of God, her eagerness—
newly formed breasts
rising, nipples peaked
and plummed—got you
carried away. You sensed the warm
pooling between her thighs and thought
of nothing else.

She said   *Taste this
and love like God* slithering tongue
over taut skin, severing flesh
with her teeth, and you could only
obey—fall down
on your knees, bow your head
and taste it.

Visions of the Messiah on Virginia Beach

Dreadlocked and beaming,
he reminded me of Jesus
fingering the heel and arch
of a new disciple

when I lifted my sandy
foot onto his thigh
and he began cleaning it
with a sun-drenched towel.

Sliding his lips
past the weak flesh
behind my knee,
he christened my calf

then gave a nod to Lazarus—
his friend with cornrows
and a boogie-board—who rose
to spread the word.

Off Season

Last night in your twin bed,
lying under the afghan

I crocheted last fall
for the coming winter,

we whispered in the dark,
afraid our voices

or the moonlight might
illuminate the past.

When you began moving
your lips toward mine

it was like confusing
a grape with an olive—

frightened, for a moment,
the taste might be bitter, overdone.

Clarification

I loved you like a hunter

    loves the precise bullet,

        the heart it stops.

            The palm's worth of blood and quick easy finish.

            The slowing blink of eyes,

                hooves, twitching, smoothing earth underneath.

I loved you like a disease

    loves an old body.

        The liver-spotted scalp, purpling veins.

        Hairbrush laced with gray strands, dead skin.

        Cancer coursing marrow, ravaging bone.

        Death's breath cooling your feet.

I loved you like a hurricane

    loves low-lying land.

        Relentless muscle of God's angry hands.

        Nails digging deep into soil, cement, idle flesh.

        Knuckles buckling brick and slate.

        Fingerprints pressed into the hearts of trees.

Shifting Ground

I am Jonah
water filling
my nose and ears
the sun lost   to fluid darkness

the tide pelting
salt into skin
my arms   useless
as driftwood

a crab scurries
through my hands   I claw
at shifting ground   searching
for an anchor of coral or seaweed

His mouth opens
and I am taken   with a school
of large silver fish   into
slippery flesh   devout bone

Genesis

Had baptismal oil balmed
his willing head, had his questions
about blood and the daughters of the earth

been answered with patience
by some angel's feathered lips,
the voices he heard with each herald's trumpet

might have colored his thoughts
magenta or indigo, not the viscous
emerald ooze of betrayal.

If Lucifer had been born instead of created,
he might have grasped the depth of a mother's
womb, of reverent longing after, of humble return.

Rite of Passage

You have made your way
through blood rivers, into revolution,
out of outstretched dying hands,
here, to my holy of holies.

My words breeze from your mouth
like laughter, like lament, like old forgotten
lies and wrap themselves
around my hungry ear.

Listening to birds cackling
from your tongue, I am afraid
my whispering might stop them mid-flight.
I remain silent as only God can—

her mouth to the ear of the world,
her hands muting their own thunder.

Aunt Jemima Meets Her Namesake in a Dream

Job 42: 12-15

I.

Imagined woman
they have given you my name,
misspelled and misplaced,
Mammy suited you better.

First second daughter of Job,
I came after the deaths, curses, boils,
the first child named in his line,
first woman he wouldn't lose
at the hands of the devil.

We were a family granted
uncommon riches, more
wealth than you've seen
on any plantation.

But they have made you plain.
Your mouth widened and scarlet
like your ordinary headdress—no crown,
no regalia sewn into your hair.
My garments bore fringes and Egyptian
blue thread. I wore no sash,
refused to be girded.

Why is your head
perpetually bowed?

Why whisper—*Yes suh, Yes suh*—
when no one is behind you
yielding a whip?

No woman smiles with lashes on her back.
Why are you stirring and singing?

II.

Imagine the beauty of my sisters
and I, unmatched by none.
Guards kept watch at my window,
stewards held men at bay near the gate.

I chose the hands
that strayed beneath
the folds of my skirt.
I wanted

the children of Israel
crowding my bones,
a man raising nations
with his hands and hips.

Men sat prostrate at my feet,
left the bed chamber chanting
my name. I was a prayer to them,
fashioned by an intimate God.

III.

Imagine the interpreter's sin,
the wrath of a slighted God—

they have misread the scrolls   distorted
'blessing'   translated 'servant' as 'slave'—

I was born into ten-fold riches,
adorned in onyx and gold

> and they present you to the world
> at a fair, in a barrel, on a box

> your hands covered in flour, face slick,
> mouth clogged with oily speech

They have forgotten
the favor I was shown

My inheritance was the same as my brothers'
My legacy was not this

Ruth v. Orpah
while traveling to Judah with Naomi

There are things I want
trust, kinship, the line of God,
a woman I am able to call mother.
Naomi has been that woman —
faithful repurchaser,
waning widow

There are things I need
rest, the full use of my youth,
a man who will make me a mother.
I thought her son was that man —
steady vessel too soon
felled by death

I lament this barren place,
the constant ache of
my fertile womb, body.
My flesh is parched, weary,
but Naomi keeps oiling my skin.
I will follow her to foreign vineyards.
I will glean, toil for food
filling emptiness

But tears are not an apology,
mourning is not sin,
this kiss, not betrayal.
I want to untie the veil of guilt.
She is with me in mind. At heart,
I yearn for the orchards of my people.
I can't forget the silence,
the absence of men

Where she goes I shall go.
Her people will be my people
and her God, my God.
Where she dies I shall die
and that is where I shall be
buried

I must go back to Moab,
my lineage, my father's fields.
Chémosh will ease my grief.
I will be a born-again woman —
more than idle flesh —
alive

Naomi Recounts Later Years With Ruth

"Do not call me Naomi. Call me Mara
for the Almighty has made it very bitter for me." – *Ruth 1: 20*

She started as a hump on my back—
heavy burden, clinging to my side.

She worked, though.
Harder than any displaced child
I'd ever seen. Could turn earth
better than every man
who stopped to watch her.

It took prodding
to coax her into Boaz's arms.
Just one night of lying
at the foot of his bed
and she turned her tongue loose
on the wrong somebody, said
Where he goes, I will go
nothing in her breath about letting life go
alongside me.

Women forget their promises
under the weight of men.

I wished them happiness,
wished them progeny,
a full marriage bed
and land just as plentiful.

But the day she bade me turn
to the fields alone, without the company
of a woman turned friend,
turned child, turned forgetful wife,
I wished them evil.

> Ruth, I wish you a turncoat-daughter
> and short-lived son.

> Boaz, son of a listless lonely mother,
> today I wish you dead.

The Mother-in-Law of Peter the Apostle
Channels Bessie Smith

Matt. 8:14, 15

Verse 1:

Find that man and ask him where he roam.
Girl, find that man and ask him where he roam.
Leave a man to Jesus and he'll never come home.

Don't have no children and you ain't practiced much.
Got no children and ain't been practicin' much.
That man done lost his mind *and* his sense of touch.

Leave your bed before dawn and sometimes you sleep alone.
He leave early in the mornin' and make you sleep alone.
Hell, even the devil know better than to leave his own.

You say you don't bother, cause Jesus make him calm.
Say you won't bother, cause Jesus brought the calm.
At night, instead of fussin', he pray and read the Psalms.

Verse 2:

What kind of man let another change his name?
What kind of man just gon' up and change his name?
Foolhearted child told me the Lord's to blame.

Gave up a good job to go and 'fish for men.'
Left his good job and his daddy to learn to 'fish for men.'
I bet when he go hungry, he'll pull them nets back in.

His brother Andrew followin' behind him, too.
Andrew say he a follower now, too.
He think the man's the son of God and what he say is true.

Simon say the heavens cleared when he dipped under water.
Jehovah opened the heavens up, when he went under water.
I ask, *What does Jesus say 'bout the way you treat my daughter?*

Verse 3:

They say he rebuke demons just by raisin' his voice.
Has the power to move demons just by liftin' his voice.
I say, *I ain't seen nothin' yet* and leave them to their choice.

Well I took sick this mornin', went to lay back down.
I couldn't stand up this mornin', had to lay back down,
but I heard the men approachin', followed by the crowd.

My body started burnin' and death was close behind.
My body filled with fire and death was close behind.
Peter entered beggin' Jesus, tellin' him it won't my time.

He laid his hand on me and the spirit flew in.
He put *one hand* on me and the spirit came in.
Jesus rid me of my fever and 'bout all my sin.

Tender

Peter says he is a shepherd
and he must tend his sheep.

His hands never strayed, before Jesus;
he turned away in the night.

He has been instructed—
Give your wife her due,

protect her from thieves, strangers—
he believes the man, and listens.

He leads with his right hand,
according to my pace.

Skin, from the scrolls, has softened his palms,
the roughness gone with the scent of sea-salt.

He summons me, and I turn
at the sound of his voice.

When I pass under the crook of his staff,
he counts me among his valuables.

My shorn hair excites him;
my plainness, he says, honors God.

He has made our bed the pasture;
I shed my garments, he calls them wool.

Praise the thrust of a man blessed
with communion, divine sight,

who names me faithful, daughter, lamb
and begins giving suck.

I am converted;
I follow him.

The Lost Gospel of Peter

I.

It is only written once
but he often called me
Satan and pushed me behind.
I think he feared my imperfection,
thought I might be the man
sent to stumble the son of God.

II.

The lame and blind
are no challenge
for one gifted with agile
feet and lucid sight
but my ailment
was dangerous, incurable—
a beastly human
long-mired in clumsy sin.

III.

The others used to watch me
for imperfection.
With each stagger or stammer,
I grew graceless in their eyes.
I wanted, so much, to be free
of mistakes—of misquoting
the scrolls, dropping
jugs of good wine—
but no day was flawless.

IV.

He was tolerant, not patient, not kind.
I got used to his biting
taught tongue, to the litany of vices
following my name.

He could have said it a thousand times—
with my feet sinking into cold sea,
my hand lax without his—
but I still wouldn't have believed
I was faithless.

V.

I tried to protect him,
but my sword was dull
and I caused the soldier much pain,
coming down three times on his ear
before shearing it off.

In front of all those men—
every one of them ready
to offer him to Caesar—
he cursed me.
Had me scour the soil for
shards of flesh
until my robes were filthy
with dirt and guilt.

All of this
when he could have lifted
the pieces from the damp earth
with his will,
without my knees
ever touching it.

VI.

He heard the cock
crowing twice before any curse
left my mouth.

He had a way
with weaknesses,
with proving simple men wrong.

I sinned
more than anyone knows
that night, not only denying him
but praying he wouldn't return.

VII.

In his final procession,
I did not walk
with Matthew or John.
I lined up behind
the children—mimicking
their steps, their open weeping—
taking pains
to pace myself home.

Notes

"Ornithology" is written for Rashad L. Williams.

"On Behalf of Frye's Grocery and the O'Jays" contains a line from the song "Darlin', Darlin' Baby" on the album *Message in the Music* recorded by the O'Jays.

"The News in Spring" is written after Marilyn Nelson and Elizabeth Alexander.

Martin Luther King III was born in 1957. His father, Dr. Martin Luther King Jr., was assassinated in 1968. His uncle, Alfred King, drowned in 1969 under mysterious circumstances, and his grandmother, Alberta Williams-King, was assassinated in church in 1974. "The Third King Dreams of Assassination" is based on these events.

In 1970, school board members in Norfolk, Virginia voted to rebuild Booker T. Washington, the only black high school in the district, in a predominantly white neighborhood. Due to student driven protests, the school board eventually ruled to rebuild on the same land. "My Mother Recalls Protests" is based on this event.

In Norfolk, Virginia most of the housing projects are named after local black leaders and end in the word *park*. "After Hurricane Isabel, Residents of Public Housing Interpret Signs" cites the names of many of these housing areas. This poem is written for Obike Reeves, Jericho Brown and Percival Everett.

During Operation Iraqi Freedom, photos were published from Abu Ghraib Prison in Iraq showing United States soldiers (male and female) demeaning and torturing Iraqi prisoners of war. "Minutes, Abu Ghraib Prison, October 18th, 2003" is based on this event.

In 2004, Simmie Knox became the first black artist ever commissioned to paint an official presidential portrait. The italicized lines in "Simmie Knox Paints Bill Clinton for the White House" are excerpts from an AP interview with the artist. This poem is written for Anita Darcel Taylor.

"Topography" is written after Tim Seibles' "Treatise."

"Rite of Passage" is written for John S. Murillo.

"Ruth v. Orpah while traveling to Judah with Naomi" is written after Tyehimba Jess.

All of the biblical quotes or verses cited in this manuscript are from the *New World Translation of the Holy Scriptures* published by the Watch Tower Bible and Tract Society of New York, Inc.

Acknowledgments

Grateful acknowledgment is given to the following publications in which some of these poems first appeared, sometimes in different versions:

"Fish Fry," *5 AM*; "Clarification," *Applesauce - Exit the Apple*; "Gesture," *Arbutus*; "The Lost Gospel of Peter" and "A Friend Explains the Second Coming," *Cave Canem Anthology IX / Bookmark Project*; "After Hurricane Isabel, Residents of Public Housing Interpret Signs," *Crab Orchard Review*; "Off Season," *Four Corners*; "Marchers Headed for Washington, Baltimore 1963," *Gathering Ground*; "Shifting Ground," *Moondance*; "Ornithology," *PMS* (poemmemoirstory); "Adam's Conversion," *The Bedside Guide to No Tell Motel*; "Visions of the Messiah on Virginia Beach," *The Bennington Review*; "1955: Snapshot in Black and White," *WarpLand–2005* Hughes, Diop, Knight Award recipient; "Minutes, Abu Ghraib Prison, October 18th, 2003," *Winning Writers–2005* Winning Writers War Poetry Contest finalist.

All praise is due to Jehovah God for his blessings and for inspiring 1 John 4:1 - "Beloved ones, do not believe every inspired expression, but test the inspired expressions to see whether they originate with God . . . ."

Eternal love and thanks to my mother, Doris D. Knight-Bingham, for setting the example and encouraging me to be who I am; to my father, Robert L. Bingham, for his strength and constant interest in my work and life; to my grandparents, great-grandparents and those who have acted as such, Mary E. Knight, Johnnie Knight, Shirley E. Bingham, Julious Bingham, Rebecca Blackburn, Viola Bingham and Loretta Bingham, for recounting our stories; to my only sister, Richelle Latisha Williams, for friendship and my favorite boy in the whole wide world; to my family, the Bingham and Knight clans, for inspiration. You are all here in some manifestation.

Much gratitude to the ancestors and present-day writers who have served as inspiration, Langston Hughes, Eloise Greenfield, Walter Dean Myers, Sharon Olds, Alicia Ostriker, Alice Mattison and countless others; to my teachers Darlene Myers, Borbie Davis, Tim Seibles, Natasha Trethewey, E. Ethelbert Miller, Ed Ochester, Amy Gerstler and Jason Shinder; to the *Callaloo* Creative Writing Workshops and its participants; to Cave Canem and all those who inspired me there, Toi Derricotte, Cornelius Eady, Sarah Micklem, Carolyn Micklem, Lucille Clifton, Kwame Dawes, Patricia Smith, Erica Hunt, Al Young, Walter Mosley, Marilyn Nelson, Cyrus Cassells, Elizabeth Alexander and Rita Dove; to the Cave Canem fellows, I wish I could name each of you, but there is no need, you are making names for yourselves.

Thank you to my dear friends and extended family, the Bennington Bitch Club, Ada Udechukwu, Anita Taylor, Jeannie Kim, David Harbilas, William Vandegrift, Jr., Sarai Walker, Kari Ruth and all other honorary members, for providing a modicum of sanity in Vermont and laughter after; to Honorée Fanonne Jeffers for love and celebration; to Eugene Calloway for becoming the kind of man your mother would have been proud of; to Jane Ahn for being my once in a lifetime friend; to my Road Dawgs, Matilda Cox and Princess Perry, there is always open road laid out before us—let's ride; to all those who have continually sustained me—light and love.

An abundance of thanks to Dr. Naomi Long Madgett for her commitment to poetry and her patience.

About the Author

Remica L. Bingham, a native of Phoenix, Arizona, received her Master of Fine Arts degree in Writing and Literature from the Writing Seminars at Bennington College. She has attended the *Callaloo* Creative Writing Workshops and is a Cave Canem fellow. In addition to other journals, her work has been featured in *5 AM*, *New Letters*, *PMS*, *Crab Orchard Review*, *Gulf Coast*, *Mosaic*, and *Essence*.

She is the recipient of the 2005 Hughes, Diop, Knight Poetry Award and was nominated for a 2005 Pushcart Prize. Currently, she is the Writing Competency Coordinator at Norfolk State University in Norfolk, Virginia. *Conversion* is her first book.